WORD GAMES for CleVer Kids

Puzzles and solutions
by Dr Gareth Moore

B.Sc (Hons) M.Phil Ph.D

Illustrations and cover
artwork by Chris Dickason

Designed by Zoe Bradley

Edited by Helen Brown

Cover Design by Angie Allison

Educational Consultancy by Kirstin Swanson

WORD GAMES for Clever Kids

Buster Books

First published in Great Britain in 2018 by Buster Books,
an imprint of Michael O'Mara Books Limited,
9 Lion Yard, Tremadoc Road, London SW4 7NQ

W www.mombooks.com/buster

f Buster Books

🐦 @BusterBooks

📷 @buster_books

Clever Kids is a trade mark of Michael O'Mara Books Limited.

Puzzles and solutions © Gareth Moore 2018

Illustrations and layouts © Buster Books 2018

A CIP catalogue record for this book is available from the British Library.

ISBN: 978-1-78055-473-0

8 10 9 7

Papers used by Buster Books are natural, recyclable products made of wood from
well-managed, FSC®-certified forests and other controlled sources. The manufacturing
processes conform to the environmental regulations of the country of origin.

Printed and bound in October 2021 by CPI Group (UK) Ltd,
108 Beddington Lane, Croydon, CR0 4YY, United Kingdom

INTRODUCTION

Are you ready to enter a whole world of wordy challenges? This book contains over 100 word games and puzzles which are designed to bamboozle the brain. Each challenge can be tackled on its own and you can work through the book at your own pace.

At the top of every page, there is a space for you to write how much time it took you to complete each game. Don't be afraid to make notes on the pages – this can be a good tactic to help you keep track of your thoughts as you work on a puzzle. There are some lined pages at the back of the book that you can use to work out your answers, too.

Read the simple instructions on each page before tackling a puzzle. If you get stuck, read the instructions again in case there's something you missed. Work in pencil so you can rub things out and have another try if you don't get the answer right the first time.

If you are still stuck, you could also try asking an adult, although did you know that your brain is actually much more powerful than a grown-up's? When you get older, your brain will get rid of lots of information it thinks it doesn't need any more, which means you might be better at solving these games than older people are.

If you're **REALLY** stuck, have a peek at the answers at the back of the book, and then try and work out how you could have got to that solution yourself.

Now, good luck and have fun!

Introducing the Word Games Master:
Gareth Moore, B.Sc (Hons) M.Phil Ph.D

Dr Gareth Moore is an Ace Puzzler, and author of lots of puzzle and brain-training books.

He created an online brain-training site called BrainedUp.com and runs an online puzzle site called PuzzleMix.com. Gareth has a Ph.D from the University of Cambridge, where he taught machines to understand spoken English.

Let the
WORD
GAMES
begin!

 TIME ....

Can you find and circle all of these swimming words in the grid to complete this wordsearch?

TOP TIP: The words may be hidden in any direction so keep your eyes peeled.

```
T D N E W O L L A H S R O H
S I L I E K O R T S K C A B
T P U W Y K E I A B T O N W
R O L S A L O D A A T S A T
E O R A G R F R E L K V T O
A L N P S N C R T E E S E O
D N L C O H I T E S P I L R
W O L U A O I H N T E E S E
A O G E N A L N T O T D N S
T D I I R R A A G A R U I D
E L I F E G U A R D B F B S
R E L O O P G N I M M I W S
B R E A S T S T R O K E L W
O S D I V I N G B O A R D S
```

BACKSTROKE   FRONT CRAWL   SPLASHING
BATHING SUIT   LANE   SWIMMING POOL
BREASTSTROKE   LIFEGUARD   TREAD WATER
BUTTERFLY   POOL NOODLE   WAVES
DEEP END   SHALLOW END
DIVING BOARD   SIDESTROKE

Rearrange the fragments on each line in order to reveal five rooms you might find in a house.

For example, OM BE DRO can be arranged to form BEDROOM.

a) DY ST U

□□□□□

b) IC TT A

□□□□□

c) HE TC N KI

□□□□□□□

d) OM BA RO TH

□□□□□□□□

e) VAT SER ORY CON

□□□□□□□□□□□□□

In each of the following sentences, write the anagram of the word written in CAPITALS in the space provided. An anagram is a word that can be made by rearranging the letters of another word.

For example, LEMONS is an anagram of MELONS.

Can you complete these anagram puzzles?

a) When I go to the swimming POOL I like to swim in

a ....

b) My .... really likes TUNA sandwiches.

c) On holiday, I sat under a PALM tree that was lit by a nearby

street ....

d) We have a .... dog that likes to play

football with my TEAM.

e) My dad thinks that APES love to eat ....

Can you find five or more words in this word circle? Each word should use the central letter 'S' plus two or more of the other letters. You can only use each letter once per word.

To help you get started, clues for three words are included below. Can you find the word that uses all six letters?

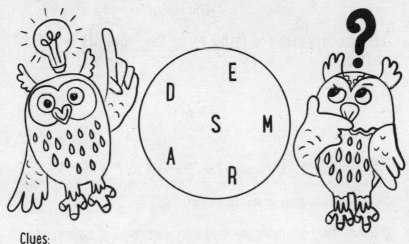

Clues:

a) Female horses ....

b) Group of male sheep ....

c) You use these to listen ....

....

....

....

....

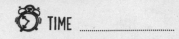
Can you decode the following two pieces of trivia? Both are written in code, but luckily in each case you've been told what the code is. The first word has been decoded to help you get started.

A B C D E F G H I J K L M N O P Q R S T U V W X Y Z

1) To read the message, shift each letter back by one. For example, change B to A, change C to B. The numbers remain the same.

Uif topx mfpqbse dbo mfbq vq up 15n – gvsuifs uibo boz puifs bojnbm.

The ....

....

2) Read this message by using the opposite of the method used to crack the previous code. If you shift past the end of the alphabet, carry on at the start of the alphabet.

Zkk ods fnkcdm gzlrsdqr zqd cdrbdmcdc eqnl z rhmfkd aqnsgdq zmc rhrsdq vgn vdqd ozhqdc azbj hm sgd 1930r.

All ....

....

....

Use your incredible brain power to climb these word ladders. All you have to do is get from the bottom to the top, filling in the gaps with new words.

Each word should use the same letters in the same order as the word below it, but with one letter changed to make a new word.

For example, you could move from CAT to DOG like this:

CAT ➡ COT ➡ DOT ➡ DOG

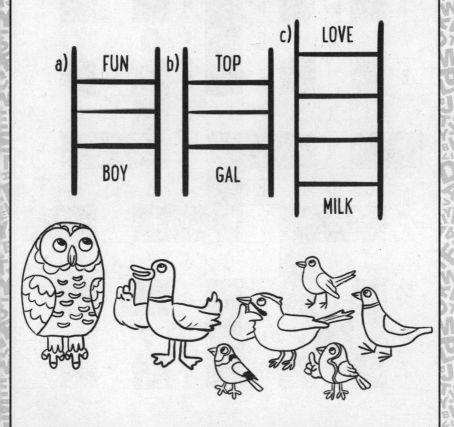

a) FUN

BOY

b) TOP

GAL

c) LOVE

MILK

Can you complete this crossword grid by adding each letter from A to Z once? Cross out each letter as you use it. Some letters have already been placed for you.

ABCDEF GHIJ~~K~~LM
NOP~~Q~~R~~S~~~~T~~UV~~W~~XYZ

L		**W**		D		M			
A		I		E		E	**Q**	A	L
B				E		M		E	
		A	M	P		O		L	O	G
		R							H
	U	D		E			A	C	H	T
A							Y	
	O	D			O	S	T	M	A	N
K				E		O			
E		T	E	R		L	L	A	
T		T		T		O		L		R

It's time to tell a story! But some of the words are missing and it's up to you to fill them in.

For each gap, write in a word that starts with the same letter of the alphabet as the items written at the bottom of the page. For example, if the item is 'your birthday month' and your birthday is in **April** then you need to find a word that starts with the letter 'A'.

Can you insert a word into each gap? It can be as sensible or as ridiculous as you like – it's completely up to you!

You have been marooned on a desert island. All you have with you is a/an ....(1). You need to build a ....(2) raft to escape. Unfortunately, you do not have any ....(3).

Luckily, you do have your trusty ....(4) with you, that is wearing ....(5).

Just as you begin to abandon hope, a/an ....(6) flies overhead and sees your brightly coloured ....(7). It sends a rescue party, and you are saved at last!

1) Your birthday month
2) Today's day of the week
3) Your age as a word
4) The current month

5) Next month
6) Your favourite colour
7) Tomorrow

Can you fit all of the listed words below into the grid opposite to make your own crossword? Three words have been added to help you get started.

3 LETTERS
Ape
Emu
Era
Eye
~~Flu~~
Hue
Kid
Mar
Opt
Ore
Rue

4 LETTERS
Club
Echo
Glee
Limb
Nest
Salt

5 LETTERS
Chick
Easel

6 LETTERS
Cherry
Create
Engine
Excuse
Forbid
Honest
Income
~~Indigo~~

7 LETTERS
~~Aquatic~~
Evening
Ostrich
Vanilla

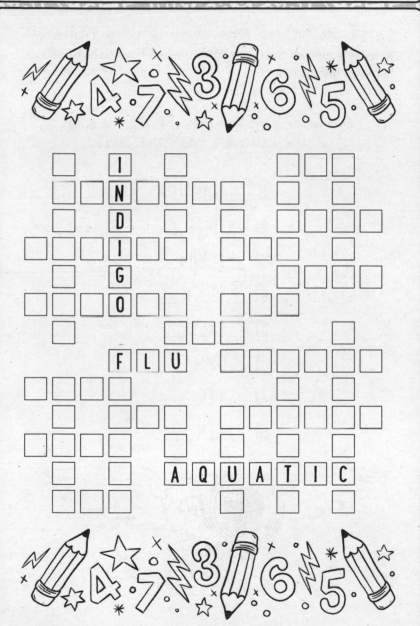

A single letter has been deleted from the start and end of each of the following words. If you know that each word starts with the same letter that it ends with, can you work out each of the missing letters and restore the original word?

For example, if you were given __NORE__ then the missing letter would be 'S', making SNORES.

1) __ARTHQUAK__

2) __TRIPE__

3) __LOWIN__

4) __IGESTE__

5) __LASSI__

6) __UMM__

7) __HEF__

8) __REN__

Can you find eight ice-cream flavours and fruit that have been hidden in this wordsearch grid?

THE RULES

You have been given the first letter of each word, as well as the number of letters it contains. You must figure out which flavour to search for, and then find the word hidden in the grid below.

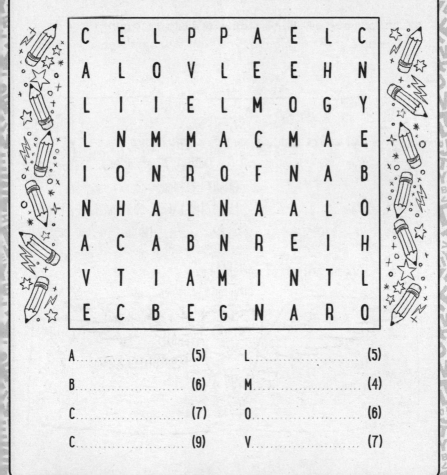

C	E	L	P	P	A	E	L	C
A	L	O	V	L	E	E	H	N
L	I	I	E	L	M	O	G	Y
L	N	M	M	A	C	M	A	E
I	O	N	R	O	F	N	A	B
N	H	A	L	N	A	A	L	O
A	C	A	B	N	R	E	I	H
V	T	I	A	M	I	N	T	L
E	C	B	E	G	N	A	R	O

A.......................... (5)   L.......................... (5)

B.......................... (6)   M.......................... (4)

C.......................... (7)   O.......................... (6)

C.......................... (9)   V.......................... (7)

You went to a fancy-dress party. The diary entry is written below but some important words have been removed. A note has been made to tell you whether the missing word is a **noun**, **adjective** or **verb**.

> A **noun** is a person, place or thing, such as 'dog'.
> An **adjective** is a describing word, such as 'red'.
> A **verb** is a doing or being word, such as 'run'.

Can you insert a **noun**, **adjective** or **verb** into each gap? It can be as sensible or as ridiculous as you like – it's completely up to you!

Last week, I went to a fancy-dress party dressed as a/an .... (NOUN). I wore a/an .... (ADJECTIVE) hat, and a/an .... (ADJECTIVE) shirt, which made me look like a/an .... (NOUN).

When I first arrived, everybody was .... (VERB), which made me .... (ADJECTIVE). I didn't expect them to .... (VERB)! It was the .... (ADJECTIVE) evening of my life.

Which of the words is the odd one out in each set and why?

1) TIGER GIRAFFE LIZARD ELEPHANT LION

....

....

2) SQUARE RHOMBUS PARALLELOGRAM
TRIANGLE RECTANGLE

....

....

3) LIME PEAS BANANA SPINACH BROCCOLI

....

....

Can you build a word pyramid on the opposite page by solving the clues? When complete, each row will spell out a word that solves its corresponding clue.

Starting from the top and working down, each layer of the word pyramid uses the same letters as the layer above it, plus one extra — although they may be in a different order.

For example, if the first layer was CAT
then the second layer could be ACTS,
and the third layer could be CARTS.

1 | C | A | T

2 | A | C | T | S

3 | C | A | R | T | S

Clues:

1) Attempt

2) You may carry food on this

3) Attend this to celebrate a birthday

4) A bakery product

Can you make four different words, each of which uses all five of the following letters on the board? There is a clue for each beneath.

For example, the letters 'A E N R S' can be rearranged to make four different words: EARNS, NEARS, SANER and SNARE.

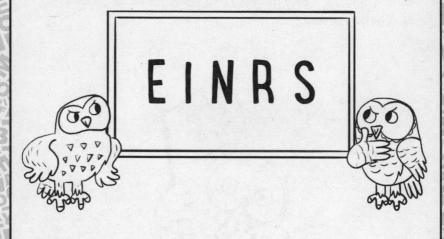

E I N R S

Clues:

a) These are used when riding a horse ....

b) You might do this when washing up ....

c) Each day, when it becomes light, then the sun has done this ....

d) Something that makes a noise on an ambulance ....

Can you draw lines to join these words into pairs to form compound words? A compound word is a word made up from two or more other words, such as 'otherwise' which can be split into 'other' and 'wise'.

Be careful, because some words have more than one possible match, but there's only one way of pairing the words up so that none are left over!

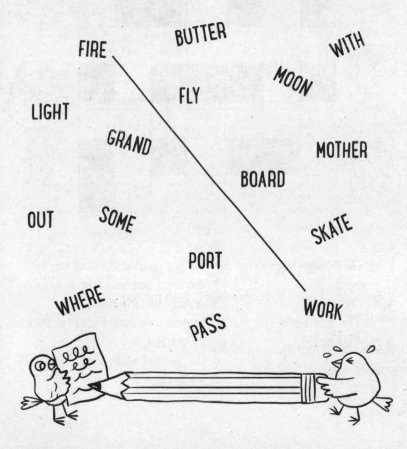

FIRE   BUTTER   WITH

MOON

FLY

LIGHT

GRAND   MOTHER

BOARD

OUT   SOME   SKATE

PORT

WHERE   WORK

PASS

Solve this crossword by writing each across and down answer in the given direction.

Can you work out the clues listed below?

Across

1. Very well-known, such as a celebrity (6)
4. Male relation (7)
6. Place to catch a train (7)
8. Musical tune (6)

Down

1. The gold medal position in a race (5)
2. You might wipe your feet on this (3)
3. Formal title for a knight (3)
5. Very dark wood, once used for black piano keys (5)
6. The result of adding some numbers (3)
7. A pair (3)

Can you have a go at solving these classic riddles?

a) What gets stuck in one place and yet travels the world?

....

b) What is used by other people more than you, even though it is yours?

....

c) What has a head but cannot talk, and a tail but cannot walk?

....

d) What has a tongue but never eats, and only ever travels in a pair?

....

The names of three body parts have been mixed up in the cauldron below. Can you rearrange the letters to spell them out? Every letter in the cauldron needs to be used, but can only be used once. Get mixing!

....

N A H G
R L A
E M D

All of the vowels have been deleted from each of the following words. Can you restore them to reveal the original words?

For example, BRNST would be BRAINIEST.

a) CLVRST .... – most intelligent

b) KNDST .... – most generous

c) GNTLY .... – softly

d) RTSTC .... – having a creative skill

e) BNNS .... – yellow fruit

The middle of the wordsearch grid is invisible! The letters are there, but you can't see them. It's your job to write them back into the grid in order to create a traditional wordsearch puzzle.

TOP TIP: Start with the longest words and work out where they must fit first.

```
F E E R H T T H I R T Y E F
O U E E E N T H E O I H E
U N E E N E E N E G E E T
R T H V S F E E V H E T U N
T V E U I I E E T E D N E E
E W I F N           T L E T E
E S Y E O           E T E F I
N V T T V           N N I F F
R Y N E N           E F I E F
E T E T T T E V D T N I N E
N F W S E N E W E E T S E E
N I T E E S T E T T V H E T
I F N T E T N E N H N I N R
E T I Y V F O R T Y N E E L
```

EIGHTEEN	FOURTEEN	THIRTY
ELEVEN	HUNDRED	THREE
FIFTEEN	NINETEEN	TWELVE
FIFTY	SEVENTEEN	TWENTY
FIVE	SIXTEEN	
FORTY	THIRTEEN	

How many words of five or more letters can you find hidden in these floating balloons? A five-letter-word has been added to help get you started. Can you find the one word that uses all of the nine letters?

TARGETS:

Good: 5 words   Excellent: 10 words   Amazing: 15 words

RAILS
....
....
....
....
....
....
....
....
....
....
....
....
....
....
....
....
....
....
....
....

Can you draw lines to join these words into pairs, so that each word is joined to a word that is its opposite?

Be careful, because some words appear twice as they have more than one possible opposite, but there's only one way of pairing the words up so that none are left over!

EASY   NO   NIGHT

YOUNG

WET

SMALL

DIFFICULT   DAY

HOT   OLD

FINISH

BLACK

DRY

HARD

YES   COLD   DARK

BIG

FIRST   WIN   WHITE

LIGHT

START   LAST

LOSE   OLD   SOFT   NEW

Can you arrange this list of words into three groups, with five words per group? Some of the words can fit into more than one group, but there is only one way of arranging them which will have exactly five words per group.

Words

Olive	Tulip	Green	Carnation
Orchid	Daisy	Magenta	Crimson
Poppy	Foxglove	Ash	Daffodil
Ruby	Gold	Blue	

Groups

Names	Flowers	Colours

....
....
....
....

Can you find a 'link word' for each pair of words? A link word is a word that can be added to the end of the first word and the start of the second word to make two new words.

For example:

QUICK  STONE

Is solved with SAND
making QUICKSAND and SANDSTONE.

1) CHEST  SHELL

2) GIRL  SHIP

Can you trace a continuous path through this grid, visiting each letter once while spelling out the list of shades of blue given beneath? To help you get started, the first word of the path is marked in for you.

```
U  Z  C  E  R  A  R  T
R  A  Y  N  I  M  A  L
E  N  A  O  I  S  E  U
P  O  W  U  H  G  I  N
R  E  D  Q  T  R  O  D
S  A  P  R  L  A  Y  I
I  H  P  U  T  L  E  M
R  E  C  E  R  U  A  N
```

AZURE
CERULEAN
CYAN
MIDNIGHT
POWDER
ROYAL
~~SAPPHIRE~~
TURQUOISE
ULTRAMARINE

Can you complete this crossword grid by adding in all of the vowels listed below? Cross out each vowel as you use it.

AAAAAAAEEEEEEEEEEEIOOOOO

S	C		S	S		R	S	
		B	N		R	M		L
	S		S					
	T	T		M	P	T		D
R							L	
K		Y	B			R	D	
	L				C			
	F			T	H		R	S

Have you ever noticed that some words have hidden numbers inside them?

For example, the word 'auditioned' contains a hidden number 'one' inside it: auditiONEd.

Can you find a word that hides each of the following numbers listed below? You only need to find one word for each number, although you might be able to find more than one if you keep trying!

a) ONE ....

b) TEN ....

c) TWO ....

d) EIGHT ....

e) NINE ....

In each of the following sentences, write the anagram of the word written in CAPITALS in the space provided. An anagram is a word that can be made by rearranging the letters of another word.

For example, LEMONS is an anagram of MELONS.

Can you complete these anagram puzzles?

a) At the beach, I saw a .... being ridden along the SHORE.

b) My toy .... has a loose PANEL that wobbles when I place it down.

c) When we go camping, my Dad .... food in the campFIRES.

d) Sometimes I lay flat on the EARTH and listen to my beating ....

e) If the .... stays overhead it COULD mean that it will rain.

f) The UNWARY animal wandered on to the ....

Delete one letter from each of the following pairs of letters to reveal five items of clothing.

For example, DC OE AP TS ➡ D̶C OE AP TS̶
reveals COAT.

a) CD LR EA ST ES ....

b) NJ EO TA TN SL ....

c) TS HA IT WR ET ....

d) PJ LA CO KN VE ST ....

e) CD EA NR ED AI TG AR SN ....

One letter is missing from each of these strange sentences. Can you work out what that letter is so that inserting it into each of the gaps will restore the original sentence? The sentences are very unusual so get your silly hat on!

For example, '__OOSE __A____LES ARE ___REAT' could have a 'G' placed in the gaps to make 'GOOSE GAGGLES ARE GREAT'.

1) __OME __E__AME __EED__ __U__TAIN __A____Y __AU__AGE __EA__ON.

2) __V__RY __GG __XP__CTS __XTR__M__ __AST__R __NT__RTAINM__NT.

3) A____ BU____S ARE I____ IN JU__Y, GENERA____Y BUT WE____ IN APRI__.

Can you find and circle all of these herbs and spices in the grid to complete this wordsearch?

TOP TIP: The words may be hidden in any direction so keep your eyes peeled.

```
E O R E G A N O H P H I L L
N I T I D P A N J O A O I D
I T O C T R F M R D R S A M
M I A D I E A S A L A O M O
S A N R N L E T M B S O D
A E Y N R R R G S U O A M S
J A E R A A E A A U P F A A
R L F D A M G O G S M F D P
A Y I I T M C O R O M R R E
E S A U U I E R N T T O A P
H T N I M M E S O L H N C P
A K I R P A P J O A R Y D E
A A N I S E E D I R O G M R
J D A S P A R S L E Y M B E
```

ANISEED   JASMINE   PARSLEY
BASIL   MINT   PEPPER
CARDAMOM   MUSTARD   ROSEMARY
FENNEL   NUTMEG   SAFFRON
GARLIC   OREGANO   TARRAGON
HORSERADISH PAPRIKA   THYME

Can you decode the following two pieces of trivia? Both are written in code, but luckily in each case you've been told what the code is. The first word has been decoded to help you get started.

A B C D E F G H I J K L M N O P Q R S T U V W X Y Z

1) To read the message, shift each letter back by five places, wrapping around from the start to the end of the alphabet. For example, change A to V, B to W, and so on.

F uzrupns nx yjhmsnhfqqd f kwzny gjhfzxj ny lwtbx kwtr ymj kqtbjwnsl ufwy tk ymj uqfsy.

A ....

....

....

2) Read this message by using the opposite of the method used to read the previous code. The numbers remain the same.

Ocz gvmbzno ampdo zqzm bmjri rvn v kphkfdi ocvo rzdbczy hjmz ocvi v hzomdx oji (1,000fb / 2,205 gwn).

The ....

....

....

A single three-letter word has been deleted from each set of three words. Can you find the missing word so that once restored to each gap you end up with three new words?

PUZZLE 1

A [ ] I V E

 F A [ ] O R

 C O M P [A] A [ ]

PUZZLE 2

V A [ ] A T E

 S [ ] E

 I N V A [ ]

Can you fit all of the listed words below into the grid opposite to make your own crossword? Two words have been added to help you get started.

3 LETTERS
Apt
Art
Ask
~~Lip~~
May
Nor
Ski
Tea

4 LETTERS
Able
Idea
Path
Sigh
Snap
Zoos

5 LETTERS
Allow
Alter
Anger
Denim
Koala
Merry
Pages
Paint
Pasta
Topic

6 LETTERS
Annual
Banana
Exotic
Giggle
Island
Legend
Orange
~~Paddle~~
Safari
Tattoo

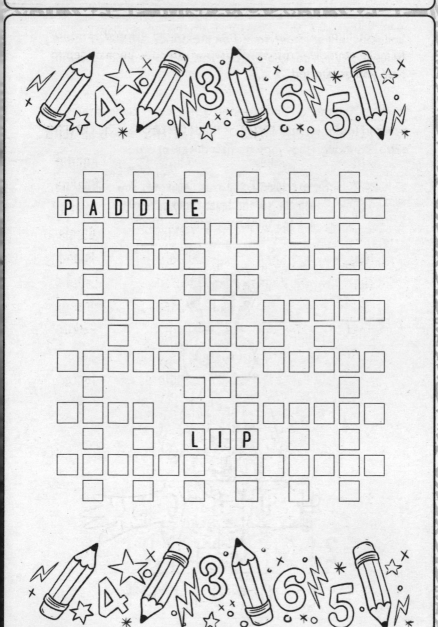

PADDLE

LIP

Can you build a word pyramid on the opposite page by solving the clues? When complete, each row will spell out a word that solves its corresponding clue.

Starting from the top and working down, each layer of the word pyramid uses the same letters as the layer above it, plus one extra – although they may be in a different order.

For example, if the first layer was DOG
then the second layer could be GOLD,
and the third layer could be LODGE.

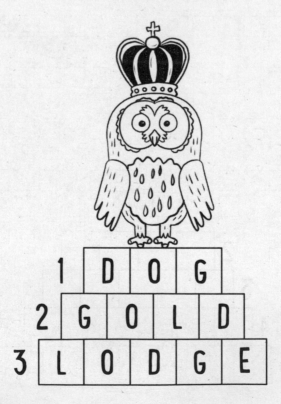

1 D O G

2 G O L D

3 L O D G E

Clues:

1) A common family pet, related to the lion

2) A horse-drawn vehicle

3) A performer on the stage or in a film

4) An orange vegetable

5) A vehicle that a farmer might use

Can you make six different words, each of which uses all six of the following letters on the board? There is a clue for each beneath.

For example, the letters 'A E N R S' can be rearranged to make four different words: EARNS, NEARS, SANER and SNARE.

A E L P S T

Clues:

a) Lightest in colour ....

b) A type of crayon ....

c) Flowers have these ....

d) You might eat from these ....

e) Folds in a skirt or other item of clothing ....

f) Used to fasten pieces of paper together ....

Solve this crossword by writing each across and down answer in the given direction.

Can you work out the clues listed below? Don't forget to time yourself!

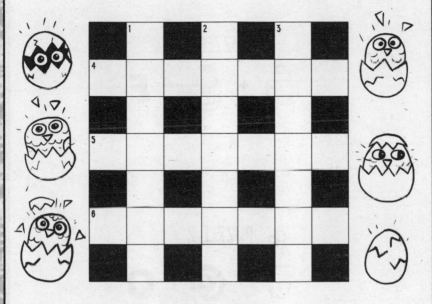

Across
4. Charged with a crime, as in 'he ____ the man of stealing' (7)
5. Personal diary (7)
6. Red, orange, yellow, green, blue, indigo and violet (7)

Down
1. Circus entertainer who leaps around (7)
2. Gentle sound made by a happy cat (7)
3. Six-sided shape (7)

Can you identify all of the following vegetables? You'll need to work out what each picture is of, and then substitute it for an appropriate word.

PUZZLE 1

+ + **E**

....

....

PUZZLE 2

+ **@** + **O**

....

....

PUZZLE 3

🚗 − **R** + **ULI** + 🌼

....

....

PUZZLE 4

B + ≡ + 🐝 − **E** + 🥫 − **C**

....

....

Rearrange the fragments on each line in order to reveal five items of household furniture.

For example, RP CA ET can be arranged to form CARPET.

a) OR RR MI

☐☐☐☐☐☐

b) AG BEA NB

☐☐☐☐☐☐☐

c) IR AR HA MC

☐☐☐☐☐☐☐☐

d) PB RD CU OA

☐☐☐☐☐☐☐☐

e) RD BE RO WA

☐☐☐☐☐☐☐☐☐

A single letter has been deleted from the start and end of each of the following words. If you know that each word starts with the same letter that it ends with, can you work out each of the missing letters and restore the original word?

For example, if you were given __NORE__ then the missing letter would be 'S', making SNORES.

1) __UESSIN__

2) __ATIO__

3) __EARL__

4) __EALT__

5) __OAS__

6) __OCA__

7) __NOW__

8) __NOC__

A list of well-known films is written below, but unfortunately some letters are missing. By inserting the missing letters, can you work out the full name of each film?

1) F_N_A_T_C _E_S_S _N_
   W_E_E _O _I_D _H_M

2) S_A_N _H_ S_E_P

3) F_N_I_G _E_O

4) T_E _E_O _O_I_

5) P_D_I_G_O_

Use your incredible brain power to climb these word ladders. All you have to do is get from the bottom to the top, filling in the gaps with new words.

Each word should use the same letters in the same order as the word below it, but with one letter changed to make a new word.

For example, you could move from CAT to DOG like this:

CAT ➡ COT ➡ DOT ➡ DOG

a)
DOG

PUP

b)
GONE

BALD

c)
MISS

TALK

⏰ TIME ....

Solve this crossword puzzle where all of the clues are given within the grid.

Grid clues:
- A person's last name
- Plural of 'loaf'
- The blackened remains of a fire
- Flying vehicle with a rotor on top
- Fruit used to make ketchup
- Width times length
- Chew food and swallow
- Retail store
- Stitched clothing border
- Evergreen tree with red berries
- Sea-based armed service
- Produce an egg, if you're a hen
- Past tense of eat
- Close your teeth on something
- Word used for agreeing
- The total amount
- Wooden barrier across land
- Farmyard animal
- Travel to and ___
- Absent from home
- Tall, round roof
- Adult human female
- Piece of wood used for rowing
- Request
- Seat covering
- Noah's per-species limit
- Slow a vehicle down
- Loud, shrill cry
- A cereal plant: an anagram of 'rey'

Can you find five or more words in this word circle? Each word should use the central letter plus two or more of the other letters. You can only use each letter once per word.

To help you get started, clues for five words are included below. Can you find the word that uses all seven letters?

Clues:

a) Bees collect this to make honey ....

b) Series of connected railway carriages ....

c) Something is close by ....

d) More pleasant ....

e) Keep hold of ....

....

....

....

....

Each of the listed words can have one of the given prefixes or suffixes attached to make a new word. Prefixes are added to the start of the word and suffixes are added to the end of the word. The first word has been completed to help you get started.

Prefixes
~~AUTO~~ OVER SEMI INTER EXTRA

AUTO........ BIOGRAPHY

.... ORDINARY

.... NATIONAL

.... CONFIDENT

.... CIRCLE

Suffixes
ABLE DOM LESS NESS SHIP

CHAMPION ....

COMFORT ....

FEAR ....

KING ....

PEACEFUL ....

The names of three safari animals have been mixed up in the cauldron below. Can you rearrange the letters to spell them out? Every letter in the cauldron needs to be used, but can only be used once. Get mixing!

....

R G T
G
F I N
A E R F
L I O I E

This crossword is different as instead of written clues an anagram of each solution word is given.

An anagram is a word that can be made by rearranging the letters of another word.

Rearrange the letters in each clue to reveal the correct word to write in the grid.

Across
2. AGRSS (5)
4. ADOORWY (7)
5. KNRTU (5)

Down
1. ACHIRTU (7)
2. TSOHG (5)
3. SNKCA (5)

Hidden somewhere in the word net below is the word 'WORDS'.
Use your brain power to find it! Start at one of the letter 'W's
and travel along the lines to connect the letters until you have
spelled out the whole word.

To see how it works, take a look at
this solved example puzzle where
'WORDS' has been spelled out:

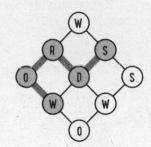

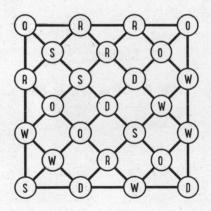

The first and last letters of some words are given below, and each set of words forms a sequence. Can you identify what each sequence is?

For example, MY, TY, WY, TY, FY would be the days of the week: MondaY, TuesdaY, WednesdaY, ThursdaY and FridaY.

Sequence 1

OE, TO, TE, FR, FE, SX

....

....

....

Sequence 2

MH, AL, MY, JE, JY, AT, SR

....

....

....

It's time to get your L-plates on! Can you find all of these school subjects in the grid? Each subject is written in the shape of an 'L'. One is solved for you to show you how it works.

TOP TIP: The words may be read either down and across, or across and up, so keep your eyes peeled.

R	R	Y	A	D	A	I	S	P	Y	I	M
C	G	H	S	R	M	H	C	G	G	G	A
T	R	P	E	A	U	S	I	C	O	N	A
A	M	A	G	M	A	I	T	H	L	S	A
R	Y	R	A	U	G	N	A	L	O	I	B
G	R	G	B	G	P	A	M	R	N	C	O
E	O	O	E	G	H	L	E	G	S	E	A
N	T	S	I	H	Y	G	H	T	A	M	T
G	L	I	S	H	S	E	B	R	A	P	A
G	P	E	I	C	I	C	S	T	D	P	A
E	M	R	H	H	E	M	I	S	T	R	Y
S	I	U	T	A	R	E	T	I	L	M	I

ALGEBRA   HISTORY
BIOLOGY   LANGUAGES
CHEMISTRY   LITERATURE
DRAMA   MATHEMATICS
ENGLISH   MUSIC
~~GEOGRAPHY~~   PHYSICS

Fancy a punt at a pun with a punchline?

Each of the following jokes is missing an important part: its punchline. Can you come up with something clever to finish each joke?

Why did the chicken become a vegetarian?

....

....

What's the difference between a cold orange and an orange cold?

....

....

Did you hear the one about the cow and the pig?

....

....

In each of the following sentences, write the anagram of the word written in CAPITALS in the space provided. An anagram is a word that can be made by rearranging the letters of another word.

For example, POT is an anagram of TOP.

Can you complete these anagram puzzles?

a) The .... adjusted its halo so it was at the correct ANGLE.

b) What do you think it MEANS that we all have different .... ?

c) The one .... I don't like about the NIGHT is that it is dark!

d) When .... howl, it sounds like they are shouting VOWELS into the air!

e) The naughty child .... the SEATED teacher.

f) When travelling, you could spend all week in a youth HOSTEL, or stay in a range of luxury ....

Can you draw lines to join these words into pairs to form compound words? A compound word is a word made up from two or more other words, such as 'otherwise' which can be split into 'other' and 'wise'.

Be careful, because some words have more than one possible match, but there's only one way of pairing the words up so that none are left over!

ALONG

BABY

BOARD

CORN

BOOK

CASE

MEAN

PAN

SHORE

KEY

SAUCE

SEA

SIDE

POP

SIT

WHILE

Can you unscramble each of these pairs of opposites?
In each case, two words have been mixed together, but each
individual word has all of its letters in the correct order.

For example, BLWAHICTKE could be written as BLACK and WHITE.

1) COGMOE ....

2) NFEAARR ....

3) OCLPOESNE ....

4) EALRALTEY ....

5) GITAVKEE ....

Can you have a go at solving these classic riddles?

a) What is lost the moment that it is shared?

....

b) What needs to feed to stay alive, but dies if given a drink?

....

c) What is full of holes and yet still holds water?

....

d) What gets left behind every time you take it?

....

Solve this crossword by writing each across and down answer in the given direction. Can you work out the clues listed below?

Across

1. Grain used for porridge (4)
4. Examination (4)
7. Currency used in many European countries (4)
8. The ____ and the Tortoise (4)
9. Celebration on 14th February, Saint ____'s Day (9)
12. Adds up (4)
14. Part of your eye; also a flower (4)
16. Free from contamination (4)
17. Substance needed to survive (4)

Down

1. The smallest whole number above zero (3)
2. Hard rock; pebble (5)
3. The blackened remains of a fire (3)
5. A motor vehicle licensed to drive passengers for payment (4)
6. In this location (4)
9. Extremely large (4)
10. Device that gives out light (4)
11. Someone who steals (5)
13. Underwater boat (3)
15. Unhappy (3)

Can you find a 'link word' for each pair of words? A link word is a word that can be added to the end of the first word and the start of the second word to make two new words.

For example:

QUICK **S A N D** STONE

is solved with SAND
making QUICKSAND and SANDSTONE.

1) ONE **S** ☐ ☐ ☐ LESS

2) POST ☐ **A** ☐ ☐ BOARD

Have you ever noticed that some words have hidden animals inside them?

For example, the word 'locate' contains a hidden 'cat' inside it: loCATe.

Can you find a word that hides each of the following animals listed below? You only need to find one word for each animal, although you might be able to find more than one if you keep trying!

a) CAT ....

b) RAT ....

c) APE ....

d) COW ....

e) PIG ....

Can you build a word pyramid on the opposite page by solving the clues? When complete, each row will spell out a word that solves its corresponding clue.

Starting from the top and working down, each layer of the word pyramid uses the same letters as the layer above it, plus one extra — although they may be in a different order.

For example, if the first layer was CAT then the second layer could be ACTS, and the third layer could be CARTS.

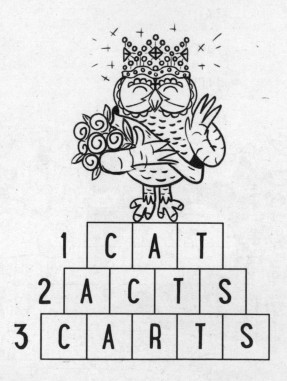

1 C A T

2 A C T S

3 C A R T S

Clues:

1) Really warm

2) A gameshow presenter

3) The opposite of 'tall'

4) Spiky parts on a plant stem

5) Special seats for kings and queens

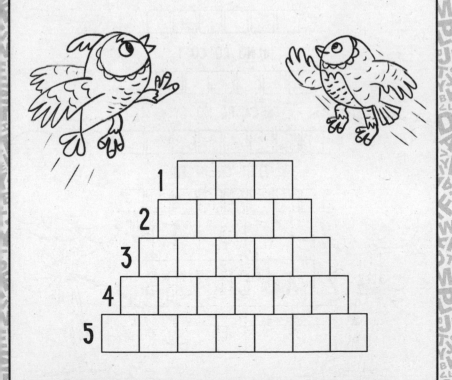

Rearrange the fragments on each line in order to reveal six types of tree.

For example, LIA NO MAG can be arranged to form MAGNOLIA.

a) PL AP E

☐☐☐☐☐

b) LL OW WI

☐☐☐☐☐☐

c) CH Y RR E

☐☐☐☐☐☐

d) NU CO CO T

☐☐☐☐☐☐☐

e) CA RE MO SY

☐☐☐☐☐☐☐☐

f) UT CH TN ES

☐☐☐☐☐☐☐☐

Can you find and circle all of these cooking utensils in the grid to complete this wordsearch?

TOP TIP: The words may be hidden in any direction so keep your eyes peeled.

M	C	R	F	G	S	B	T	P	S	P	O	O	N
N	C	E	U	O	P	N	E	S	S	P	U	C	K
L	A	M	E	C	R	E	A	G	P	N	C	N	N
E	C	P	L	N	L	K	H	P	I	L	I	L	I
E	S	N	E	E	S	P	G	T	L	F	A	E	S
F	E	N	R	C	S	F	E	N	E	L	R	T	L
A	E	K	L	E	U	K	L	A	T	R	I	W	E
S	O	O	C	N	A	A	E	P	S	P	O	R	E
I	E	W	W	C	S	E	S	K	E	B	P	P	G
E	O	G	A	R	L	I	C	P	R	E	S	S	C
V	F	R	E	N	E	P	O	E	L	T	T	O	B
E	E	C	R	E	H	S	A	M	A	S	T	E	S
T	P	A	P	P	L	E	C	O	R	E	R	G	S
L	L	I	R	R	E	L	A	D	L	E	P	L	R

APPLE CORER   FORK   MASHER   SIEVE
BOTTLE OPENER   GARLIC PRESS   MUG   SPOON
BOWL   GRILL PAN   PEELER   WOK
CAKE TIN   KNIFE   PLATE
CUP   LADLE   SAUCEPAN

Can you fit all of the listed words below into the grid opposite to make your own crossword? The first word has been added to help you get started.

3 LETTERS
Egg
Red

4 LETTERS
Drag
Earl
Hard
Item
Rage
Stag

5 LETTERS
Above
Agree
Green
Idiot
Talon
Title
Truth
Utter

6 LETTERS
Common
Depart
Infect
Little

7 LETTERS
Silence
Student
Toddler
Vehicle

8 LETTERS
Elephant
Ointment

9 LETTERS
Afternoon
Entertain

VEHICLE

⏲ TIME ....

How many words of five or more letters can you find hidden in these floating balloons? A five-letter-word has been added to help get you started. Can you find the one word that uses all of the nine letters?

TARGETS:
Good: 5 words   Excellent: 10 words   Amazing: 15 words

PATIO

....
....
....
....
....
....
....
....
....
....
....
....
....
....

....

....

....

A single letter has been deleted from the start and end of each of the following words. If you know that each word starts with the same letter that it ends with, can you work out each of the missing letters and restore the original word?

For example, if you were given __NORE__ then the missing letter would be 'S', making SNORES.

1) __LAYGROU__

2) __HUNDERBOL__

3) __EMINDE__

4) __ESIGNE__

5) __OPSCOTC__

6) __COUT__

7) __ROM__

8) __DG__

Can you crack this coded crossword? Every letter from A-Z has been assigned a different value, and every square in the crossword grid contains a value. It's up to you to work out which letter matches which value, and fill in the grid accordingly. Don't forget to time yourself!

THE RULES

Two words have already been written in to get you started. BACK, for example, shows that 10=B, 11=A, 23=C and 19=K. Start by looking through the grid for everywhere that these numbers appear, and write in the corresponding letters. For example, the second square on the top row is an 11, so write in 'A'. Then repeat with the other given word. To solve the rest of the puzzle you'll need to use all of your word and code-cracking skills!

TOP TIP: Keep track of the code with the boxes beneath the puzzle, and use the letters around the sides to keep track of which letters you've already used.

TIME ....

~~A~~		6	11	4	4	9	21	24		10 B	11 A	23 C	19 K	~~N~~
~~B~~	18		2		14		9			20		14		O
~~C~~	22	11	17	9	18		3	11	12	12	9	21	7	P
D	11		9		9		9		14			6		Q
~~E~~	5 M	9 E	7 N	26 U		2	11	25	25	14	2	20	4	R
F	3		12		11		12		25		11			S
G		1	26	9	18	12		15	9	11	7	18		T
H			21		12		25		9		6		18	~~U~~
I	18	8	9	3	8	9	21	2		13	9	21	14	V
J		9			5		20		18		21		23	W
~~K~~	18	11	26	18	11	6	9		23	4	14	23	19	X
L		17		20			7		11		26		18	Y
~~M~~	4	24	7	16		11	2	2	21	9	18	18		Z

1	2	3	4	5	6	7	8	9	10	11	12	13
				M		N		E	B	A		

14	15	16	17	18	19	20	21	22	23	24	25	26
					K				C			U

TIME ....

Can you trace a continuous path through this grid, visiting each letter once while spelling out the list of shades of purple given beneath? To help you get started, the first word of the path is marked in for you.

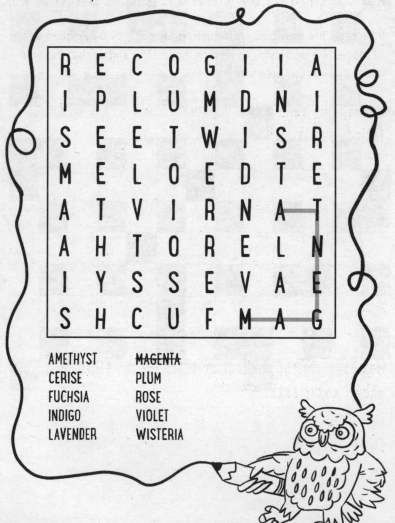

R	E	C	O	G	I	I	A
I	P	L	U	M	D	N	I
S	E	E	T	W	I	S	R
M	E	L	O	E	D	T	E
A	T	V	I	R	N	A	T
A	H	T	O	R	E	L	N
I	Y	S	S	E	V	A	E
S	H	C	U	F	M	A	G

AMETHYST	~~MAGENTA~~
CERISE	PLUM
FUCHSIA	ROSE
INDIGO	VIOLET
LAVENDER	WISTERIA

Can you decode the following two pieces of trivia? Each has been written in code, and it's up to you to work out what the exact code is.

A B C D E F G H I J K L M N O P Q R S T U V W X Y Z

1) To read the message, shift each letter back by a certain number of places. It's up to you to work out what the shift is, but the first word is written to help you.

Nenah hnja, xena 650 vruurxw kxccunb xo Qnrwi Cxvjcx Tnclqdy jan bxum fxaumfrmn.

Every ....

....

....

2) To read the message, shift each letter forward by a certain number of places. It's up to you to work out what the shift is, but the first word is written to help you.

Max Exzh vhfitgr vnkkxgmer ftdxl tuhnm 40 ubeebhg ukbvdl xoxkr rxtk.

The ....

....

....

A list of well-known children's books is written below, but unfortunately some letters are missing. By inserting the missing letters, can you work out the full name of each book?

1) T__E C__T __N __H__ H__T

2) __H__ L__O__, T__E __I__C__ A__D
   __H__ W__R__R__B__

3) A__I__E__ A__V__N__U__E__ I__
   W__N__E__L__N__

4) __H__R__I__ A__D __H__
   C__O__O__A__E __A__T__R__

5) W__N__I__ T__E __O__H

6) T__E __O__B__T

There's a vowel thief on the loose! All the vowels in the following fruits have been stolen. Can you find the missing vowels to reveal the original words?

For example, BNN would be BANANA.

a) PPL ....

b) PLM ....

c) RNG ....

d) PR ....

e) MLN ....

f) LM ....

g) PRCT ....

h) MNG ....

Can you find ten sports that have been hidden in this wordsearch grid?

THE RULES

You have been given the first letter of each word, as well as the number of letters it contains. You must figure out which sport to search for, and then find the word hidden in the grid below.

```
L B L R U N N I N G
L A L L B E S H N O
A D A I A I N I C G
B M B Y N B M A N N
Y I T N R M T I W H
E N E N I E L O O S
L T K W L C H C O I
L O S A Y T K C I F
O N A C A E S U R I
V A B O Y S A W K A
```

A.................... (7)   H.................... (6)

B.................... (9)   R.................... (7)

B.................... (10)   S.................... (8)

C.................... (7)   T.................... (6)

F.................... (8)   V.................... (10)

A single three-letter word has been deleted from each set of three words. Can you find the missing word so that once restored to each gap you end up with three new words?

PUZZLE 1

C H ☐ ☐ T E D

S H ☐ ☐ T E R

☐ H ☐ ☐ C H

PUZZLE 2

☐ O ☐ T A G E

M A S ☐ O ☐

☐ ☐ O ☐ T O N

Can you arrange this list of words into four groups, with four words per group? Some of the words can fit into more than one group, but there is only one way of arranging them which will have exactly four words per group.

Words

Ace	Duchess	Earl	Diamond
Prince	Square	Baronet	Club
Spade	Wrench	Heart	Circle
King	Queen	Axe	Joker

Groups

Tools	Playing Cards	Nobles	Shapes

....

....

....

....

Hidden somewhere in the word net below is the word 'SEARCH'. Use your brain power to find it! Start at one of the letter 'S's and travel along the lines to connect the letters until you have spelled out the whole word.

To see how it works, take a look at this solved example puzzle where 'WORDS' has been spelled out:

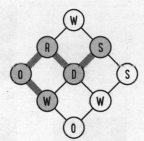

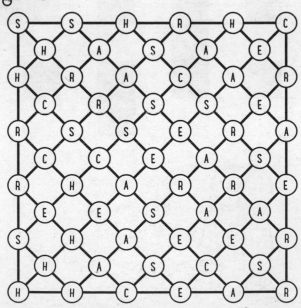

Solve this crossword by writing each across and down answer in the given direction.

Can you work out the clues listed on the opposite page?

Across
1. Small bang (3)
3. Powder used for making chocolate drinks (5)
6. Move in time to music (5)
7. Head motion used for agreeing (3)
8. Roman warrior who fought in public displays (9)
9. Bite (like a small dog) (3)
10. Common type of cat with dark stripes (5)
12. Each one of something (5)
13. Chew and swallow (3)

Down
1. Peas grow in this (3)
2. Large tropical fruit with tough, spiky skin (9)
3. Science subject (9)
4. Police officer responsible for keeping the peace (9)
5. Small, poisonous snake that's native to Britain (5)
8. Magical spirit, sometimes found in a lamp (5)
11. So far (3)

Can you find eight or more words in this word circle? Each word should use the central letter plus two or more of the other letters. You can only use each letter once per word.

To help you get started, clues for five words are included below. Can you find the two words that use all eight letters?

Clues:

a) Consuming food ....

b) Imaginary being of human form but superhuman size ....

c) A number less than 10 ....

d) A hinged barrier used to prevent entry ....

e) Period of darkness ....

....

....

....

....

Use your incredible brain power to climb these word ladders. All you have to do is get from the bottom to the top, filling in the gaps with new words.

Each word should use the same letters in the same order as the word below it, but with one letter changed to make a new word.

For example, you could move from CAT to DOG like this:

CAT ➡ COT ➡ DOT ➡ DOG

a)

MAD

RUN

b)

COLD

WARM

c)

WANT

JOKE

⏰ TIME ....

In each of the following sentences, write the anagram of the word written in CAPITALS in the space provided. An anagram is a word that can be made by rearranging the letters of another word.

For example, POT is an anagram of TOP.

Can you complete these anagram puzzles?

a) This large .... I have is SUPER!

b) My TUTOR told me that at the weekend he likes to fish for

....

c) I developed a SENSOR to detect when my sleeping brother

.... !

d) The greengrocer made a .... promise that he would start selling MELONS.

e) The shopkeeper TAGGED the .... so that it would not be stolen.

f) Some strange BLEATS came from the .... where only horses were supposed to be!

Delete one letter from each of the following pairs of letters to reveal six countries of the world.

For example, EC ON AG LS AQ NT PD ➡ E̶C O̶N A̶G L̶S̶ A̶Q N̶T P̶D̶ reveals ENGLAND.

a) GJ AH EP NA ND ....

b) IC MN AD TI EA ....

c) CI LH AI MN RA ....

d) TS LP OA TI EN ....

e) CB RL EA VZ OI NL ....

f) GF RE RA PN CA TE ....

Can you find all of these birds in the grid? Each bird is written in the shape of an 'M'. One is solved for you to show you how it works.

TOP TIP: The words may read either left to right or from right to left so keep your eyes peeled.

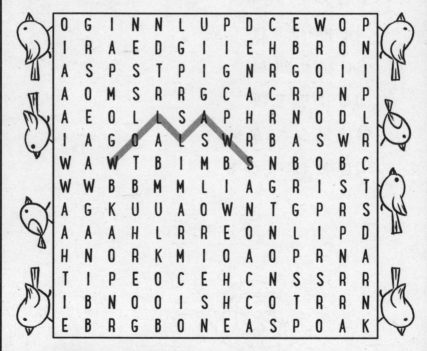

```
O G I N N L U P D C E W O P
I R A E D G I I E H B R O N
A S P S T P I G N R G O I I
A O M S R R G C A C R P N P
A E O L L S A P H R N O D L
I A G O A L S W R B A S W R
W A W T B I M B S N B O B C
W W B B M M L I A G R I S T
A G K U U A O W N T G P R S
A A A H L R R E O N L I P D
H N O R K M I O A O P R N A
T I P E O C E H C N S S R R
I B N O O I S H C O T R R N
E B R G B O N E A S P O A K
```

ALBATROSS	HUMMINGBIRD	SPARROW
CHICKEN	OSTRICH	STORK
CORMORANT	PENGUIN	~~SWALLOW~~
GOOSE	ROBIN	WAGTAIL
HERON	SANDPIPER	

Can you unscramble each of these pairs of opposites?
In each case, two words have been mixed together, but each
individual word has all of its letters in the correct order.

For example, BLWAHICTKE could be written as BLACK and WHITE.

1) HCOOLTD ....

2) FSASLOTW ....

3) PPUSULHL ....

4) BWEORSTST ....

5) AASWLAEKEPE ....

The first and last letters of some words are given below and each set of words forms a sequence. Can you identify what each sequence is?

For example, MY, TY, WY, TY, FY would be the days of the week: MondaY, TuesdaY, WednesdaY, ThursdaY and FridaY.

Sequence 1

RD, OE, YW, GN, BE, IO, VT

....

....

....

Sequence 2

FT, SD, TD, FH, FH, SH, SH

....

....

....

The names of three colours have been mixed up on the artist's easel below. Can you rearrange the letters to spell them out? Every letter on the easel needs to be used, but can only be used once. Get out your colour palette!

....

U
R
N
E
R
L
L
B
G
P
E
E
E
P
U

Can you build a word pyramid on the opposite page by solving the clues? When complete, each row will spell out a word that solves its corresponding clue.

Starting from the top and working down, each layer of the word pyramid uses the same letters as the layer above it, plus one extra – although they may be in a different order.

For example, if the first layer was CAT
then the second layer could be ACTS,
and the third layer could be CARTS.

1 C A T

2 A C T S

3 C A R T S

Clues:

1) Help

2) Past tense of say

3) Thoughts

4) Group of women

5) Small points

6) In a regular and even manner

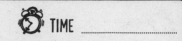
Try out your poetry skills by completing these two-line poems. The first line of each poem is given to you, but the second is missing. If you can, try to come up with something that rhymes.

Every day I think aloud,

....

At certain times of year I say,

....

If flowers could walk they'd surely move,

....

Which of the words is the odd one out in each set and why?

1) RIGHT   WRONG   OBTUSE   ACUTE   REFLEX

....

....

2) LEMON   ORANGE   PEACH   LIME   GRAPEFRUIT

....

....

3) EGGS   BUTTER   CHEESE   CREAM   YOGURT

....

....

Solve this crossword by writing each across and down answer in the given direction.

The 'across' clues are anagrams. Rearrange the letters in each of these clues to reveal the correct word to write in the grid.
The 'down' clues are regular crossword clues.

Can you work out the clues listed on the opposite page?

Across
1. AEMRSSTT (8)
5. ILO (3)
6. ABEMR (5)
8. AEIIMNPTT: Hint: Not wanting to wait for something (9)
10. EENRV (5)
13. AGT (3)
15. AEKLMRUW: Hint: Neither hot or cold (8)

Down
1. Sound made by a cow (3)
2. Colourful spring flower that grows from a bulb (5)
3. Tall tree with broad, oval-shaped leaves (3)
4. Use your eyes (3)
6. A person performing in a play (5)
7. Rodent that resembles a large mouse (3)
8. Small hotel, often in the countryside, providing food and drink (3)
9. More of something (5)
11. Snake-shaped fish (3)
12. Sound to express alarm, surprise or horror (3)
14. Precious stone (3)

There's a vowel thief on the loose! All the vowels in the following adjectives have been stolen. Can you find the missing vowels to reveal the original words?

For example, PLYFL would be PLAYFUL.

1) PRPL ....

2) SCRY ....

3) WLD ....

4) TLL ....

5) KND ....

6) YNG ....

7) NRST ....

8) SMRT ....

Can you decode the following two pieces of trivia? Each one has been written in code, and it's up to you to work out what the exact code is.

1) Can you work out how to read this message? If you get stuck, try thinking about where the spaces should really go.

Pig eon sca nre mem ber peo ple byt hei rfa ces and soo nle arn toc ome tot hos ewh ofe edt hem and avo idt hos ewh och ase the maw ay.

....

....

....

2) Can you work out how to read this message? If you get stuck, it might help to look at it from a different point of view.

.dnuorg eht stih fooh s'esroh eht nehw kcohs eht brosba spleh tl !gorf a dellac si fooh s'esroh a fo htaenrednu ehT

....

....

....

....

Can you make five different words, each of which uses all six of the following letters? There is a clue for each beneath.

For example, the letters 'A E N R S' can be rearranged to make four different words: EARNS, NEARS, SANER and SNARE.

Don't worry if you can't get all five – one or two of them are tricky words that you might not know!

E I L N S T

Clues

a) You use your ears to do this ....

b) Not making any sound ....

c) A type of Christmas decoration ....

d) To join the army ....

e) Narrow arms of a sea, lake or river ....

A story is written below but some important words have been removed. A note has been made to tell you whether the missing word is a noun, adjective or verb.

A noun is a person, place or thing, such as 'dog'.
An adjective is a describing word, such as 'red'.
A verb is a doing or being word, such as 'run'.

Can you insert a noun, adjective or verb into each gap? It can be as sensible or as ridiculous as you like — it's completely up to you!

Today I bought a/an ....(ADJECTIVE)
.... (NOUN). I chose it because I
.... (VERB) its ....
(ADJECTIVE) ....(NOUN)! That's one of
my favourite things, along with its ....
(ADJECTIVE) .... (NOUN).

I took it home, where it was great to ....
(VERB). Now I keep it with my ....
(ADJECTIVE) .... (NOUN) in a corner of
my room.

Can you fit all of the listed words below into the grid opposite to make your own crossword? The first word has been added to help you get started.

3 LETTERS
Air
Die
Eat
Too

5 LETTERS
Awake
Enemy
Habit
Nurse
Saint
Story
Straw
Trips

6 LETTERS
Asleep
Eraser
Errand
Pirate
Powder
Remedy
Renews
Temple

7 LETTERS
Peacock
Toaster
Weather
Whisker

9 LETTERS
Blackbird
Honeymoon
~~Marmalade~~
Spaghetti

M A R M A L A D E

TIME ....

How many words of five or more letters can you find hidden in these floating balloons? A five-letter-word has been added to help get you started. Can you find the one word that uses all of the nine letters?

TARGETS:
Good: 5 words   Excellent: 10 words   Amazing: 15 words

DIGIT

Can you draw lines to join these words into pairs to form homophone pairs? Homophones are words that sound the same when spoken, but have different meanings or spellings. For example, 'pear' and 'pair' are homophones.

Be careful, because some words have more than one possible match, but there's only one way of pairing the words up so that none are left over!

AISLE   AURAL   CENSOR   EWE

EYELET   HOLE   CUE   ISLE

KNOT

ISLET   YEWS

KNOWS   KNIGHT

SCENE

NOT   NOSE

ONE   NIGHT

SEIZE

QUEUE   RING

ORAL   SEAS   YOU   SENSOR

SEEN   USE

WHOLE   WON   WRING

Have you ever noticed that some words have hidden colours inside them?

For example, the word 'admired' contains a hidden 'red' inside it: admiRED.

Can you find a word that hides each of the following colours listed below? You only need to find one word for each colour, although you might be able to find more than one if you keep trying!

a) RED ....

b) TAN ....

c) ASH ....

d) LIME ....

e) ROSE ....

Can you find a 'link word' for each pair of words? A link word is a word that can be added to the end of the first word and the start of the second word to make two new words.

For example:

QUICK S A N D STONE

is solved with SAND
making QUICKSAND and SANDSTONE.

1) FORT  ☐ ☐ ☐ H ☐ FALL

2) GRAND M ☐ ☐ ☐ ☐ ☐ MIND

Can you complete this crossword grid by adding each letter from A to Z once? Cross out each letter as you use it.

ABCDEFGHIJkLM NOPQRSTUVWXYZ

S	P		E	R	E			E		I	T
O				E							H
		R			R	O		I	S		
N		I		L							F
	I		Z			F	E		S		
		O						N			
	A	N		O				I	T	A	
L							I		I		I
U		D	R	E	S		S		I		
E								U		H	
S	O			S	T		E	E	T		

Can you draw lines to join these words to form compound words? A compound word is a word made up from two or more other words, such as 'otherwise' which can be split into 'other' and 'wise'.

Be careful, because some words have more than one possible match, but there's only one way of pairing the words up so that none are left over!

BALL

COMB

CROSS

BODY

EYE

GOWN

FALL

BACK

FORT

KEY

HERO

HOLE

HONEY

SOME

NIGHT

OVER

WATER

SIGHT

PACK

SUPER

Can you identify all of the following vehicles? You'll need to work out what each picture is of and then substitute it for an appropriate word.

PUZZLE 1

 – **D**

....

....

PUZZLE 2

T +

....

....

PUZZLE 3

PUZZLE 4

B + (coat) − C

PUZZLE 5

(bull) + (sleeping man zzz) + R

A list of countries is written below, but unfortunately some letters are missing. Can you work out the full name of each of these countries?

1) __N__T__D __T__T__S

2) __U__T__A__I__

3) S__I__Z__R__A__D

4) C__N__D__

5) __O__T__ A__R__C__

6) __E__ Z__A__A__D

Can you find all of the listed shapes in the grid? Each word is written in a spiral. One is solved for you to show you how it works.

TOP TIP: The words always read outwards from the centre of the spiral, but the spiral may start by moving up, right, down or left, so keep your eyes peeled.

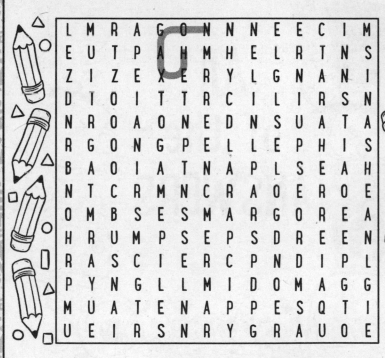

L	M	R	A	G	O	N	N	N	E	E	C	I	M
E	U	T	P	A	H	M	H	E	L	R	T	N	S
Z	I	Z	E	X	E	R	Y	L	G	N	A	N	I
D	I	O	I	T	T	R	C	I	L	I	R	S	N
N	R	O	A	O	N	E	D	N	S	U	A	T	A
R	G	O	N	G	P	E	L	L	E	P	H	I	S
B	A	O	I	A	T	N	A	P	L	S	E	A	H
N	T	C	R	M	N	C	R	A	O	E	R	O	E
O	M	B	S	E	S	M	A	R	G	O	R	E	A
H	R	U	M	P	S	E	P	S	D	R	E	E	N
R	A	S	C	I	E	R	C	P	N	D	I	P	L
P	Y	N	G	L	L	M	I	D	O	M	A	G	G
M	U	A	T	E	N	A	P	P	E	S	Q	T	I
U	E	I	R	S	N	R	Y	G	R	A	U	O	E

CYLINDER   PARALLELOGRAM   SPHERE

DIAMOND   PENTAGON   SQUARE

ELLIPSE   PYRAMID   TRAPEZIUM

~~HEXAGON~~   RECTANGLE   TRIANGLE

OCTAGON   RHOMBUS

All
of the
ANSWERS

WORD GAME 1

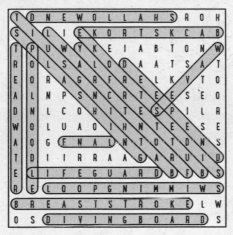

WORD GAME 2

a) STUDY

b) ATTIC

c) KITCHEN

d) BATHROOM

e) CONSERVATORY

WORD GAME 3

a) When I go to the swimming POOL I like to swim in a LOOP.

b) My AUNT really likes TUNA sandwiches.

c) On holiday, I sat under a PALM tree that was lit by a nearby street LAMP.

d) We have a TAME dog that likes to play football with my TEAM.

e) My dad thinks that APES love to eat PEAS.

WORD GAME 4

a) MARES
b) RAMS
c) EARS

Other words include (but are not limited to): ads, arms, dames, dams, dares, dears, eras, mars, mas, reads, reds, sad, same, sea, seam, sear and smear.

The word that uses all of the letters is **DREAMS**.

WORD GAME 5

1) The snow leopard can leap up to 15m – further than any other animal.

2) All pet golden hamsters are descended from a single brother and sister who were paired back in the 1930s.

WORD GAME 6

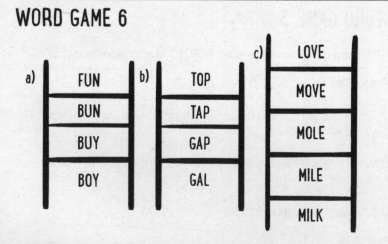

a)
FUN
BUN
BUY
BOY

b)
TOP
TAP
GAP
GAL

c)
LOVE
MOVE
MOLE
MILE
MILK

WORD GAME 7

```
L   W   D   M   D   F
A L I V E   E Q U A L
B   Z   E   M   E   I
S H A M P O O   L O G
    R     R         H
J U D G E   Y A C H T
A       X       Y
C O D   P O S T M A N
K   A   E   O   B   E
E N T E R   L L A M A
T   E   T   O   L   R
```

WORD GAME 9

```
  E   I   G       H U E
  V A N I L L A   O   A
  E   D   E   P   N E S T
E N G I N E   E Y E   E
  I   G       S A L T
I N C O M E   O P T
  G       M A R       O
    F L U   E X C U S E
E C H O       R     T
  H   R U E   C H E R R Y
L I M B   R   L   A   I
  C   I   A Q U A T I C
  K I D   B   E   H
```

WORD GAME 10

1) E: EARTHQUAKE   5) C: CLASSIC
2) S: STRIPES   6) Y: YUMMY
3) G: GLOWING   7) T: THEFT
4) D: DIGESTED   8) A: ARENA

WORD GAME 11

APPLE   LEMON
BANANA   MINT
CARAMEL   ORANGE
CHOCOLATE   VANILLA

WORD GAME 13

1) **Lizard** is the odd one out as all of the other animals are mammals.
2) **Triangle** is the odd one out as all of the other shapes have four sides.
3) **Banana** is the odd one out as the other foods are green in colour.

WORD GAME 14

1) TRY
2) TRAY
3) PARTY
4) PASTRY

WORD GAME 15

a) REINS
b) RINSE
c) RISEN
d) SIREN

WORD GAME 16

BUTTERFLY
FIREWORK
GRANDMOTHER

MOONLIGHT
PASSPORT
SKATEBOARD

SOMEWHERE
WITHOUT

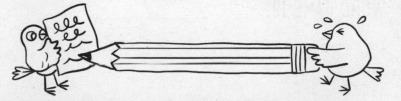

WORD GAME 17

	F	A	M	O	U	S
	I		A			I
B	R	O	T	H	E	R
	S				B	
S	T	A	T	I	O	N
U			W		N	
M	E	L	O	D	Y	

WORD GAME 18

a) A stamp
b) Your name
c) A coin
d) A shoe

WORD GAME 19

The three parts of the body are: arm, hand and leg.

WORD GAME 20

a) CLEVEREST
b) KINDEST
c) GENTLY
d) ARTISTIC
e) BANANAS

WORD GAME 21

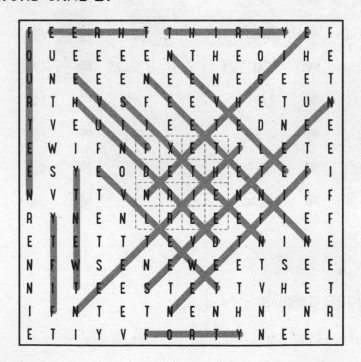

WORD GAME 22

Words of five or more letters include (but are not limited to): artist, altruist, lairs, liars, lotus, orals, rails, ratio, riots, roast, ritual, solar, stair, start, stilt, stout, strait, suitor, tarot, tarts, toast, total, touts, trait, trial, trios, trots, trout, trust, tutors, tailor, tourist.

The word that uses all of the letters is TUTORIALS.

WORD GAME 23

BIG	➡ SMALL		NIGHT	➡ DAY
BLACK	➡ WHITE		OLD	➡ NEW
EASY	➡ DIFFICULT		START	➡ FINISH
FIRST	➡ LAST		WET	➡ DRY
HARD	➡ SOFT		WIN	➡ LOSE
HOT	➡ COLD		YES	➡ NO
LIGHT	➡ DARK		YOUNG	➡ OLD

WORD GAME 24

Names: Ash, Daisy, Olive, Poppy, Ruby

Flowers: Carnation, Daffodil, Foxglove, Orchid, Tulip

Colours: Blue, Crimson, Green, Gold, Magenta

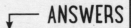

WORD GAME 25

1) NUT, to make CHESTNUT and NUTSHELL

2) FRIEND, to make GIRLFRIEND and FRIENDSHIP

WORD GAME 26

WORD GAME 27

S	C	I	S	S	O	R	S	
	O		E		A		E	
	A	B	N	O	R	M	A	L
	S		S			E		E
A	T	T	E	M	P	T	E	D
R		R	O		E		L	
K	E	Y	B	O	A	R	D	
	L		A		C		E	
F	E	A	T	H	E	R	S	

WORD GAME 28

Words that contain a hidden number include (but are not limited to):

a) ONE: alone, anyone, ballooned, bone, cone, done, phone, tone

b) TEN: antenna, attend, brighten, contend, detention, extend, intend, mitten, written

c) TWO: artwork, footwork, network, outwore, stuntwoman, trustworthy

d) EIGHT: freight, height, sleight, weight

e) NINE: canine, boniness, feminine, funniness, mezzanine, sunniness

WORD GAME 29

a) At the beach, I saw a **HORSE** being ridden along the SHORE.

b) My toy **PLANE** has a loose PANEL that wobbles when I place it down.

c) When we go camping, my Dad **FRIES** food in the campFIRES.

d) Sometimes I lay flat on the EARTH and listen to my beating **HEART**.

e) If the **CLOUD** stays overhead it COULD mean that it will rain.

f) The UNWARY animal wandered on to the **RUNWAY**.

WORD GAME 30

a) DRESS
b) JEANS
c) SHIRT
d) JACKET
e) CARDIGAN

WORD GAME 31

1) S: Some sesame seeds sustain sassy sausage season.

2) E: Every egg expects extreme Easter entertainment.

3) L: All bulls are ill in July, generally, but well in April.

WORD GAME 32

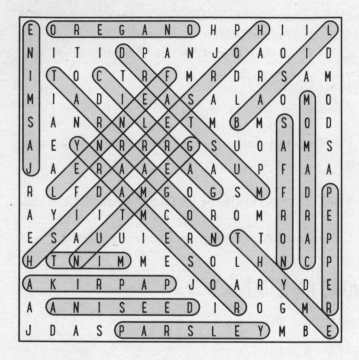

WORD GAME 33

1) A pumpkin is technically a fruit because it grows from the flowering part of the plant.

2) The largest fruit ever grown was a pumpkin that weighed more than a metric ton (1,000kg / 2,205 lbs).

WORD GAME 34

Puzzle 1: ACT, to make ACTIVE, FACTOR and COMPACT
Puzzle 2: LID, to make VALIDATE, SLIDE and INVALID

WORD GAME 35

```
  B     I  D     M     Z     G
P A D D L E     E X O T I C
  N     E     N O R     R     O     G
  S A F A R I     R     S I G H
  N         M A Y             L
P A S T A     N     A L T E R
    K     P A G E S     E
P A I N T     E     K O A L A
    N         A R T             E
S N A P     L     O R A N G E
    U     A     L I P     B     E
T A T T O O     I S L A N D
    L     H     W     C     E     D
```

WORD GAME 36

1) CAT
2) CART
3) ACTOR
4) CARROT
5) TRACTOR

WORD GAME 37

a) PALEST   d) PLATES
b) PASTEL   e) PLEATS
c) PETALS   f) STAPLE

WORD GAME 38

	A		P		H	
A	C	C	U	S	E	D
	R		R		X	
J	O	U	R	N	A	L
	B		I		G	
R	A	I	N	B	O	W
	T		G		N	

WORD GAME 39

Puzzle 1: CAB + BAG + E = CABBAGE
Puzzle 2: POT + AT + O = POTATO
Puzzle 3: CAR – R + ULI + FLOWER = CAULIFLOWER
Puzzle 4: B + ROAD + BEE – E + CAN – C = BROAD BEAN

WORD GAME 40

a) MIRROR   d) CUPBOARD
b) BEANBAG   e) WARDROBE
c) ARMCHAIR

WORD GAME 41

1) G: GUESSING
2) N: NATION
3) Y: YEARLY
4) H: HEALTH
5) T: TOAST
6) L: LOCAL
7) S: SNOWS
8) K: KNOCK

WORD GAME 42

1) *FANTASTIC BEASTS AND WHERE TO FIND THEM*
2) *SHAUN THE SHEEP*
3) *FINDING NEMO*
4) *THE LEGO MOVIE*
5) *PADDINGTON*

WORD GAME 43

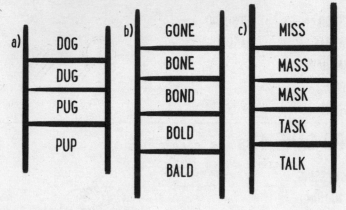

a)
DOG
DUG
PUG
PUP

b)
GONE
BONE
BOND
BOLD
BALD

c)
MISS
MASS
MASK
TASK
TALK

WORD GAME 44

	S		L		A		T	
	U		O		S	H	O	P
A	R	E	A		H	E	M	
	N	A	V	Y		L	A	Y
	A	T	E		B	I	T	E
	M		S			C	O	W
Y	E	S		F	R	O		
		U		E		P	A	D
W	O	M	A	N		T	W	O
	A		S	C	R	E	A	M
B	R	A	K	E		R	Y	E

WORD GAME 45

a) NECTAR
b) TRAIN
c) NEAR
d) NICER
e) RETAIN

Other words include (but are not limited to): ant, antic, can, cane, canter, certain, crane, enact, inert, neat, net, nice, nit, rain, ran, rant, recant, rein, rent, retina, tan, ten, tin, and trance.

The word that uses all of the letters is **CERTAIN**.

WORD GAME 46

Prefixes:
AUTOBIOGRAPHY, EXTRAORDINARY, INTERNATIONAL, OVERCONFIDENT, SEMICIRCLE

Suffixes:
CHAMPIONSHIP, COMFORTABLE, FEARLESS, KINGDOM, PEACEFULNESS

WORD GAME 47

The three safari animals are: **giraffe, lion** and **tiger**.

WORD GAME 48

			H			
	G	R	A	S	S	
	H		I		N	
D	O	O	R	W	A	Y
	S		C		C	
	T	R	U	N	K	
			T			

WORD GAME 49

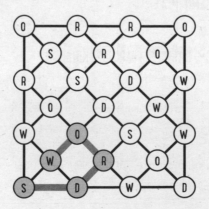

WORD GAME 50

Sequence 1 are numbers: OnE, TwO, ThreE, FouR, FivE, SiX

Sequence 2 are months: MarcH, ApriL, MaY, JunE, JulY, AugusT, SeptembeR

WORD GAME 51

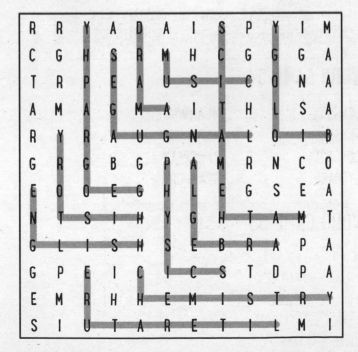

R	R	Y	A	D	A	I	S	P	Y	I	M
C	G	H	S	R	M	H	C	G	G	G	A
T	R	P	E	A	U	S	I	C	O	N	A
A	M	A	G	M	A	I	T	H	L	S	A
R	Y	R	A	U	G	N	A	L	O	I	B
G	R	G	B	G	P	A	M	R	N	C	O
E	O	O	E	G	H	L	E	G	S	E	A
N	T	S	I	H	Y	G	H	T	A	M	T
G	L	I	S	H	S	E	B	R	A	P	A
G	P	E	I	C	I	C	S	T	D	P	A
E	M	R	H	H	E	M	I	S	T	R	Y
S	I	U	T	A	R	E	T	I	L	M	I

WORD GAME 53

a) The **ANGEL** adjusted its halo so it was at the correct **ANGLE**.

b) What do you think it **MEANS** that we all have different **NAMES**?

c) The one **THING** I don't like about the **NIGHT** is that it is dark!

d) When **WOLVES** howl, it sounds like they are shouting **VOWELS** into the air!

e) The naughty child **TEASED** the **SEATED** teacher.

f) When travelling, you could spend all week in a youth **HOSTEL**, or stay in a range of luxury **HOTELS**.

WORD GAME 54

ALONGSIDE   MEANWHILE
BABYSIT   POPCORN
BOOKCASE   SAUCEPAN
KEYBOARD   SEASHORE

WORD GAME 55

1) COME and GO
2) NEAR and FAR
3) OPEN and CLOSE
4) EARLY and LATE
5) GIVE and TAKE

WORD GAME 56

a) A secret
b) A fire
c) A sponge
d) A footstep

WORD GAME 57

O	A	T	S		A		
N			T	E	S	T		H
E	U	R	O		H	A	R	E
			N			X		R
V	A	L	E	N	T	I	N	E
A		A			H			
S	U	M	S		I	R	I	S
T		P	U	R	E			A
		B		F	O	O	D

WORD GAME 58

1) SELF, to make ONESELF and SELFLESS
2) CARD, to make POSTCARD and CARDBOARD

WORD GAME 59

Words that contain a hidden animal include (but are not limited to):

a) CAT: allocate, catacomb, catalogue, catch, cater, communicate, intricate, placate, scatter
b) RAT: accurate, admiration, brat, bureaucrat, crate, decorate, narrate, rate
c) APE: agape, aperture, apex, cape, chapel, drape, paper, shape, tape
d) COW: coward, cower, cowl, ecowarrior, scowl
e) PIG: epigram, pigeon, pigment

WORD GAME 60

1) HOT
2) HOST
3) SHORT
4) THORNS
5) THRONES

WORD GAME 61

a) APPLE
b) WILLOW
c) CHERRY
d) COCONUT
e) SYCAMORE
f) CHESTNUT

WORD GAME 62

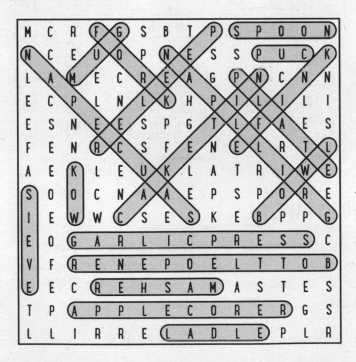

WORD GAME 63

```
    V E H I C L E   R A G E
  U   N   T   I     E   R
  T I T L E   T O D D L E R
  T   E   M   T   E     E
  E A R L   E L E P H A N T
  R   T   C   E   A     F
    T A L O N   T R U T H
    I   M   I   T   E   A
  O I N T M E N T   D R A G
    D   O   F   H   N   R
  S I L E N C E   A B O V E
    O   G   C   R   O   E
  S T A G   S T U D E N T
```

WORD GAME 64

Words of five or more letters include (but are not limited to):
aioli, allot, atoll, atopic, aplitic, calli, coalpit, iliac, italic, licit,
lilac, local, octal, optic, optical, patio, pilot, plait, politic, topic,
topical.

The word that uses all of the letters is **POLITICAL**.

WORD GAME 65

1) P: PLAYGROUP
2) T: THUNDERBOLT
3) R: REMINDER
4) D: DESIGNED

5) H: HOPSCOTCH
6) S: SCOUTS
7) A: AROMA
8) E: EDGE

WORD GAME 66

	G	A	L	L	E	R	Y		B	A	C	K
S		D		O		E			I		O	
W	A	V	E	S		P	A	T	T	E	R	N
A		E		E		E		O			G	
M	E	N	U		D	A	F	F	O	D	I	L
P		T		A		T		F		A		
	Q	U	E	S	T		J	E	A	N	S	
	R		T		F		E		G			S
S	H	E	P	H	E	R	D		Z	E	R	O
	E		M		I			S		R		C
S	A	U	S	A	G	E		C	L	O	C	K
	V		I		E			A		U		S
L	Y	N	X		A	D	D	R	E	S	S	

Q	D	P	L	M	G	N	H	E	B	A	T	Z
O	J	X	V	S	K	I	R	W	C	Y	F	U

WORD GAME 67

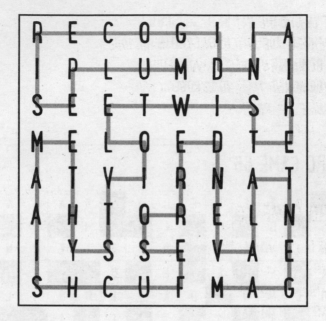

WORD GAME 68

1) To decode the message, shift each letter back by nine places to reveal:
Every year, over 650 million bottles of Heinz Tomato Ketchup™ are sold worldwide.

2) To decode the message, shift each letter forward by seven places to reveal:
The Lego™ company currently makes about 40 billion bricks every year.

WORD GAME 69

1) *THE CAT IN THE HAT*
2) *THE LION, THE WITCH AND THE WARDROBE*
3) *ALICE'S ADVENTURES IN WONDERLAND*
4) *CHARLIE AND THE CHOCOLATE FACTORY*
5) *WINNIE THE POOH*
6) *THE HOBBIT*

WORD GAME 70

a) APPLE   e) MELON
b) PLUM   f) LIME
c) ORANGE   g) APRICOT
d) PEAR   h) MANGO

WORD GAME 71

ARCHERY
BADMINTON
BASKETBALL
CYCLING
FOOTBALL

HOCKEY
RUNNING
SWIMMING
TENNIS
VOLLEYBALL

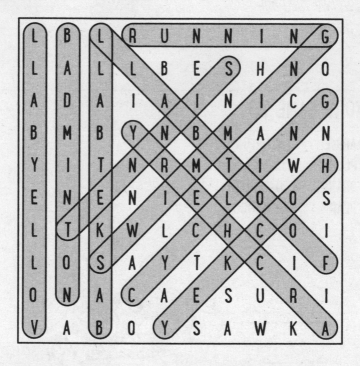

WORD GAME 72

PUZZLE 1: HAT, to make CHATTED, SHATTER and HATCH

PUZZLE 2: COT, to make COTTAGE, MASCOT and COTTON

WORD GAME 73

Tools: Axe, Club, Spade, Wrench
Playing Cards: Ace, Joker, King, Queen
Nobles: Baronet, Duchess, Earl, Prince
Shapes: Circle, Diamond, Heart, Square

WORD GAME 74

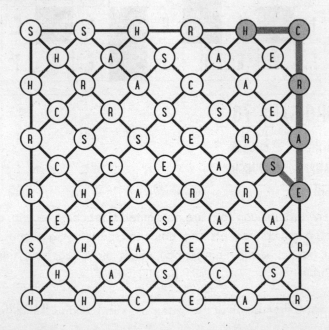

WORD GAME 75

P	O	P		C	O	C	O	A
O		I		H		O		D
D	A	N	C	E		N	O	D
		E		M		S		E
G	L	A	D	I	A	T	O	R
E		P		S		A		
N	I	P		T	A	B	B	Y
I		L		R		L		E
E	V	E	R	Y		E	A	T

WORD GAME 76

a) EATING   d) GATE
b) GIANT   e) NIGHT
c) EIGHT

Other words include (but are not limited to): aching, acting, age, agent, cage, change, etching, gain, gait, gent, get, gin, gnat, hag, hang, hating, heating, hinge, nag, neigh, night, tag, tang, thing and tinge.

The words that use all of the letters are CHEATING and TEACHING.

WORD GAME 77

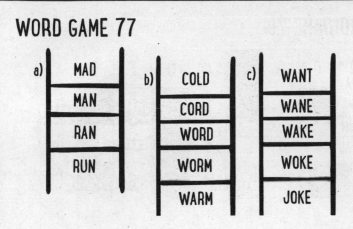

a) MAD / MAN / RAN / RUN

b) COLD / CORD / WORD / WORM / WARM

c) WANT / WANE / WAKE / WOKE / JOKE

WORD GAME 78

a) This large PURSE I have is SUPER!

b) My TUTOR told me that at the weekend he likes to fish for TROUT.

c) I developed a SENSOR to detect when my sleeping brother SNORES!

d) The greengrocer made a SOLEMN promise that he would start selling MELONS.

e) The shopkeeper TAGGED the GADGET so that it would not be stolen.

f) Some strange BLEATS came from the STABLE where only horses were supposed to be!

WORD GAME 79

a) JAPAN
b) INDIA
c) CHINA
d) SPAIN
e) BRAZIL
f) FRANCE

WORD GAME 80

WORD GAME 81

1) HOT and COLD
2) FAST and SLOW
3) PUSH and PULL
4) BEST and WORST
5) AWAKE and ASLEEP

WORD GAME 82

Sequence 1 are colours of the rainbow: ReD, OrangE, YelloW, GreeN, BluE, IndigO, VioleT

Sequence 2 are positions ('ordinal' numbers): FirsT, SeconD, ThirD, FourtH, FiftH, SixtH, SeventH

WORD GAME 83

The three colours are: blue, green and purple.

WORD GAME 84

1) AID
2) SAID
3) IDEAS
4) LADIES
5) DETAILS
6) STEADILY

WORD GAME 86

1) **Wrong** is the odd one out as all of the rest are types of mathematical angle.

2) **Peach** is the odd one out as the rest are all citrus fruits.

3) **Eggs** is the odd one out as the the rest are all made from milk.

WORD GAME 87

M	A	T	T	R	E	S	S	
O		U			L		E	
O	I	L		A	M	B	E	R
		I		C				A
I	M	P	A	T	I	E	N	T
N				O		X		
N	E	V	E	R		T	A	G
	E		E			R		E
	L	U	K	E	W	A	R	M

WORD GAME 88

1) PURPLE
2) SCARY
3) WILD
4) TALL
5) KIND
6) YOUNG
7) NEAREST
8) SMART

WORD GAME 89

1) The spaces have been rearranged so the letters are grouped into sets of three. By rearranging the spaces you can reveal:
Pigeons can remember people by their faces and soon learn to come to those who feed them and avoid those who chase them away.

2) Read all of the text backwards, starting at the end and reading back to the beginning, to reveal:
The underneath of a horse's hoof is called a 'frog'! It helps absorb the shock when the horse's hoof hits the ground.

WORD GAME 90

a) LISTEN
b) SILENT
c) TINSEL
d) ENLIST
e) INLETS

WORD GAME 92

```
R E N E W S   T E M P L E
E   U   E   S   N   E   R
M A R M A L A D E   A I R
E   S   T   I   M   C   A
D I E   H O N E Y M O O N
Y       E   T       C   D
  S T O R Y   A W A K E
A   O       S   H       P
S P A G H E T T I   T O O
L   S   A   R   S   R   W
E A T   B L A C K B I R D
E   E   I   W   E   P   E
P I R A T E   E R A S E R
```

WORD GAME 93

Words of five or more letters include (but are not limited to): digit, diner, dirge, during, dieting, editing, grind, grunt, guide, guider, inter, ignite, intrude, nudge, reign, ridge, rigid, riding, ringed, ruined, tiger, tined, tinge, tired, tuned, tuner, tidier, tiding, tinged, tinier, tiring, trudge, turned, under, unite, untie, urged, urine, united, untied, urgent.

The word that uses all of the letters is **INTRIGUED**.

WORD GAME 94

AISLE	➡	ISLE	NIGHT ➡ KNIGHT
AURAL	➡	ORAL	ONE ➡ WON
CUE	➡	QUEUE	SCENE ➡ SEEN
EWE	➡	YOU	SEAS ➡ SEIZE
HOLE	➡	WHOLE	SENSOR ➡ CENSOR
ISLET	➡	EYELET	USE ➡ YEWS
KNOT	➡	NOT	WRING ➡ RING
KNOWS	➡	NOSE	

WORD GAME 95

Words that contain a hidden colour include (but are not limited to):

a) RED: bred, credit, acquired, barred, tired
b) TAN: acceptance, assistant, blatant, botanic, stand, tango
c) ASH: bash, cash, dash, flash, rash, sash, wash
d) LIME: compliment, limerick, millimetre, slime, sublime
e) ROSE: arose, microsecond, morose, prosecutor

WORD GAME 96

1) NIGHT, to make FORTNIGHT and NIGHTFALL
2) MASTER, to make GRANDMASTER and MASTERMIND

WORD GAME 97

S	P	H	E	R	E	■	E	X	I	T
O	■	O	■	E	■	■	■	■	■	H
U	■	R	■	P	R	O	M	I	S	E
N	■	I	■	L	■	F	■	■	■	F
D	I	Z	Z	Y	■	F	E	A	S	T
■	■	O	■	■	■	■	■	N	■	■
B	A	N	J	O	■	V	I	T	A	L
L	■	■	W	■	■	I	■	I	■	I
U	N	D	R	E	S	S	■	Q	■	G
E	■	■	■	■	■	I	■	U	■	H
S	O	C	K	■	S	T	R	E	E	T

WORD GAME 98

BACKPACK	HONEYCOMB
BALLGOWN	KEYHOLE
CROSSOVER	SOMEBODY
EYESIGHT	SUPERHERO
FORTNIGHT	WATERFALL

WORD GAME 99

Puzzle 1: CARD − D = CAR
Puzzle 2: T + RAIN = TRAIN
Puzzle 3: HAIR − H + C + RAFT = AIRCRAFT
Puzzle 4: B + COAT − C = BOAT
Puzzle 5: BULL + DOZE + R = BULLDOZER

WORD GAME 100

1) UNITED STATES
2) AUSTRALIA
3) SWITZERLAND
4) CANADA
5) SOUTH AFRICA
6) NEW ZEALAND

WORD GAME 101

```
L M R A G O N N N E E C I M
E U T P A H M H E L R T N S
Z I Z E X E R Y L G N A N I
D T O I T T R C I L I R S N
N R O A O N E D N S U A T A
R G O N G P E L L E P H I S
B A O I A T N A P L S E A H
N T C R M N C R A O E R O E
O M B S E S M A R G O R E A
H R U M P S E P S D R E E N
R A S C I E R C P N D I P L
P Y N G L M I D O M A G G
M U A T E N A P P E S O T I
U E I R S N R Y G R A U O E
```

The end!

Well done

NOTES
AND
SCRIBBLES

NOTES AND SCRIBBLES ⟶

NOTES AND SCRIBBLES →

NOTES AND SCRIBBLES

NOTES AND SCRIBBLES

ARE YOU READY FOR YOUR NEXT CHALLENGE?

ISBN 9781780557106

ISBN 9781780557403

ISBN 9781780555638

ISBN 9781780556659

ISBN 9781780556642

ISBN 9781780556192

ISBN 9781780556185

ISBN 9781780556628

ISBN 9781780555935

ISBN 9781780555621

ISBN 9781780556635

ISBN 9781780556543

ISBN 9781780554723

ISBN 9781780555409

ISBN 9781780556208

ISBN 9781780553146

ISBN 9781780553078

ISBN 9781780553085

ISBN 9781780552491